U THE COSTUME

Poems

NANCY O'SHAUGHNESSY

Outskirts Press, Inc.
Denver, Colorado

Outskirts Press, Inc.
http://www.outskirtspress.com

ISBN: 978-1-4327-2159-6

Outskirts Press and the "OP" logo are trademarks belonging to Outskirts Press, Inc.

PRINTED IN THE UNITED STATES OF AMERICA

Please accept this humble offering of original poems
in loving memory of my grandparents:

Herman and Sadie Ratz
&
Kenneth and Leone Sauer

A writer writes not because he is educated but because he is driven by the need to communicate. Behind the need to communicate is the need to share. Behind the need to share is the need to be understood. The writer wants to be understood much more than he wants to be respected or praised or even loved. And that perhaps, is what makes him different from others.

Leo C. Rosten

TABLE OF CONTENTS

FUGITIVE

We all perish.
Will you be remembered?
Is there any evidence of your existence?
Or did you just take up space?
Will thoughts of you cross someone's mind?
Will your name be spoken through someone's lips?
Will they search for your star in heaven's sky?
Leave your imprint.
Time is a fleeting fugitive.

JUDGE AND JURY

The veil covers the woman's face.
It hides nothing.
Isolated she knows what she sees.
Her eyes see life through romantic eyes.
A sheer curtain falls to the ground.
The barrier is almost invisible.
It is meant to keep them apart.
Never to be a whole but two halves.
The distance is eternal.
In her imagination she weeps.
Don't judge her.
The verdict returned is not guilty.
No crime has been committed.
The actions don't match the words.
You say one thing but she hears another.
Maybe love is a crime.
Another leads you away in cuffs.
The woman's arms cannot reach you.
You whisper through her life like a ghost.

FATE

He is unaware.
But he has the power to both save and destroy you.
You are wandering too near the edge.
With each step forward the ground disintegrates.
You inch closer and closer to self destruction.
Like a car crash you are unable to look away.
Your field of vision narrows.
You look to see what he is feeling.
So many questions you cannot ask.
You read between the lines.
Hoping to hear what he is not saying.
Despair and hope fight within you.
A padlocked heart hides a tormented temptress.
Obsessed and possessed.
Your fate came too late.

FALLING SNOW

Frozen tears from heaven.
The snowflakes flutter and fall.
Swirl and drift.
There is no warmth under this white blanket.
It covers everything.
Each small leaf is accessorized in white.
A beauty that is deceiving.
Like many people.
It is beautiful but cold.
It has no substance.
It is slippery.
You try to hold it and it is gone.

NEW YORK COUPLE

It was an innocent event.
The day their hearts met.
He was with her.
She was with him.
Legal documents signed years ago.
But their hearts sang to each other.
Their souls recognized the truth.
They listened to what nature intended.
Now they are together.
A love publicly announced in <u>The New York Times</u>.
That part may have been a mistake.
Many judge the love story.
How could she do that?
How could he do that?
Without being asked, opinions are offered.
Cruel words are said.
Few understand the truth.
But the heart leads where it will.
It goes where it must go.
True love will not be harnessed.
It needs the other half that makes it whole.

DAMSEL IN DISGRACE

Who are you even?
Beyond recognition.
Fallen woman in the making.
You must stay strong.
Say all the right things.
Convince yourself.
It's not true.
But your heart is not listening.
It feels what it feels.
Making no excuses.
You eat in denial.
Not because of hunger.
But to keep your mouth full.
If you don't watch yourself.
Maybe no one else will either.
Then you would be safe.
Do you go left or do you go right?
A heart will be broken.
Yours or mine.

QUIET MAN

Thank you.
No more for me.
This quiet is an abuse.
I can no longer bear to hear.
Still waters may run deep.
But I am drowning.

WISHING WELL

Years have passed since I stood clutching the coins.
Hands filled to overflowing.
Fast as lightening I flung each coin into the well.
Over the edge I peered.
Hello, anyone?
I'm waiting.
So many wishes made before mine.
Did any come true?
Leaning too far forward I tumbled into the well.
At the bottom I landed.
From there I could see the brightness of the sun.
But I could not feel its warmth.
It is always constant; yesterday, today, tomorrow.
Now I see you standing at the edge.
You hope your wish will come true.
Over and over it is the same wish.
It is only a different face whose lips utter the wish.
We all wish for love.
Wish you well.

MY HEART

For my son, Patrick

Did you know I slipped my heart into your pocket?
You are carrying it everywhere you go.
With every step of your journey it is there.
Silently it is pressed against you.
It is with you when you wake up.
And it is with you when you go to sleep.
It is exactly where it is meant to be.
The minute you were born it belonged to you.

PRETENDER

Paste on that smile.
Make small talk.
You are the perfect actress.
Pretend you are what you are not.
Vibrant and alive.
Once upon a time
I was like you.
Optimistic and full of hope.
Sunny and carefree.
Young and beautiful.
A million years ago.
Another time.
Another place.
Things change.
You will see.

LAST HOPE

It is the end.
With all her strength she clutches the stone cross.
The nails on her fingers are torn and bleeding.
Her arms scrapped raw.
She is so cold.
Her mind is numb.
The wave tries to wash her away.
It tosses her down like a broken doll.
She is being pulled to pieces.
Still she clings to the cross.
It is her last hope.

SHELTER DOG

In the dark the computer screen glows.
All of you look back at me.
You with your sad little dog faces.
Silently your eyes plead.
Please, please, please, pick me.
Give me a chance.
I need you.
Come for me.
You know you are a really good dog.
How can they not see that?
The cute little puppies will always find a home.
But the ones who are a little older may not.
Time may run out.
There are just so many of you.

You break my heart.
So much need.
Forever homes wanted.
A place that is safe just for you.
You have a lot of love to wrap around a family.
Rescues, shelters, animal cavalries, pet angels.
The various websites tell your brief tragic life story.
Without you your owner moved away.
I don't understand that ignorance.
Abandoned, abused and starving.
Discarded like trash and left by the dumpster.
It breaks my heart seeing you like that.
Knowing what you have needlessly endured.
How can I choose one of you over another?
I want to save all of you.

GROWN OLD

With your scrunched-up face you walk ahead.
Head down, marching along.
Who cares if she is beside or behind you?
Where she is or what she does no longer matters.
As she has aged you have grown bored with her.
She is an afterthought at this point.
What you once felt for her is dead.
Evaporated and gone.
She tries to reach your brittle dried-up heart.
You were her lover and friend.
Her hand you once held.
Now you just take up space in her bed.
No talking.
No touching.
It is not her loss.
It is yours.

STEP RIGHT UP

The time has come.
You walk out.
The door gently closes behind you.
Fresh air hits your face.
This is not the end.
It is the beginning.
It is a new chapter in your life book.
Roll the dice.
Move your peg around the game board.
Away you go.
Step right up.
The whistle blows.
The train departs the station.
Your new dreams wait ahead.

PHONY

You look perfect.
First class all the way.
You greet me with a "Hello. How are you?"
But before I can speak you have already turned away.
Your time is too valuable to wait for my reply.
My smile is frozen on my face.
Slowly it slips off.
I was right you are first class.
Only it is a first class phony.

BLIND SPOT

There they are.

They sit on the ground.

Their backs pressed against the concrete wall.

Their hands reach towards you.

Fingers outstretched.

You turn your head away.

Look how thin they are.

Are they starving?

Now that is a weight loss plan.

Why should you give them your hard earned money?

They will probably just buy booze.

Well maybe not the ones with the kids.

You have so much.

Should you share?

You don't think so.

Not going to happen.

If you give to them there won't be enough for you.

Pretend that you are talking on your phone.

You are so important.

You just put them in your blind spot.

They are invisible.

Now you see them.

Now you don't.

SEARCHING

Where are you?
You must be searching for me.
I'm looking into every face for you.
I will feel it.
I will know.
The stars will be aligned.
Angels will sing.
I will know when it is you.
Some have thought they were you.
They pretended.
But it didn't last.
Separately our years are going by quickly.
Time is running out for us.
But I will search for you until my last day.

MASTERPIECE

On the easel the canvas sits.
His yesterday lover sketched in pencil.
With eyes that stare straight through him.
Teasing and mocking.
A love sacrificed.
Love and hate.
Two sides of the mirror reflected.
The artist slaps and scrapes the paint across the canvas.
He smears the paint to the very edges.
Blobs drip to the floor.
Paint covers his hands.
And coats the brush handle.
But it is not enough.
Armed with his palette knife;
he slashes the canvas to shreds.
They could have been a masterpiece.

LOVE AT FIRST SIGHT

For my dog, Nicky

In the photograph I saw your face.
Your smile reached my eyes.
My heart was struck by Cupid's arrow.
I knew I had to have you.
It was love at first sight.
In my hands you slipped away.
But even death can't stop this love.
I will always love you.

GOODBYE MY NICKY

Goodbye my dear friend.
Just for now.
No time at all.
Fate wouldn't let it be forever.
I hope the memories you take with you are all happy.
You are and have been loved so much by me.
My heart couldn't hold all the love I felt for you.
I hope that you have felt that love every day of your life.
You have made every day of my life better.
Right now my heart has never felt so broken.
And I have never cried so many tears.
Please forgive me those times that I was short with you.
It was never really you I was upset with.
You just needed to be close to me and wanted my attention.
Thank you for always listening to me without judging me.
Your kind and gentle ways will guide me the rest of my days.
There are many of our loved ones in heaven.
I know they will scoop you up and love you like crazy until I
can again.
Someday we will be together again my sweet boy.
And we'll walk side by side in the sunshine.
You have been the best dog ever!
I love you my Nicky.

REFLECTION

Propped on the table the mirror rests.
I sit and stare.
Who is that?
No one I recognize.
The reflection looking back is not me.
Not who I want to be nor who I set out to be.
A pile of clay that no hands have formed.
The faded photograph.
A dented can.
Peeling paint.
An as-is piece.
The sell date long past.
Slow to smile.
A heart bruised black and blue.
Silent decisions are pondered.
Before weariness or weakness consume me.
There is much work to do.

SHARKS

Just hold still.
Don't move a muscle.
Stay right where you are.
They are circling.
Sharks are everywhere.

HEARTACHE

You make my heart hurt.
It is always the same.
I should know by now.
I never learn.
Why do I allow you that power over me?
I wouldn't with anyone else.
I would walk away.
And never look back.
Your name would be erased off my list.
You focus in on my vulnerabilities.
My weak spots exposed.
Slowly you try to bring me to my knees.
Still I love you.
My hope is that someday you will really know me.
And just love me.
No strings attached.

PINK PETALS

At her feet they fall.
Blush pink petals.
Smooth as velvet.
Their leafy green stems discarded.
The dirt begins to show as her garden grows bare.
Over and over each flower is wished upon.
And as each petal is plucked she chants:
"He loves me."
"He loves me not."
Again and again she whispers the same words.
"Will he ever love me?"

LOCKED-IN

She appears normal.
On the surface there is nothing out of the ordinary.
Nothing screams damaged goods.
No alarms going off.
No flashing red lights.
Her rhetoric is pretty average.
She laughs and cries in all the right places.
Useless tears destroy a perfectly made up face.
Nothing indicates she is lost inside herself.
She stands in the middle of her world.
Falling at her feet the sides come crashing down.
The shadows close in.
Mindlessly medicated.
Locked-up tight.
Alone.

DREAM DAY

I think I will lie in this grass for a while.
And ponder and pretend I'm a princess at play.
Warmed by the sun the ground gathers me close.
Each blade of grass is velvety soft.
For my eyes alone the clouds put on a show.
Gently the wind whispers to me.
A lullaby composed to ease me to sleep.
Behind my closed lids a dream begins.
A day like today will make you believe.
That sometimes your dreams do come true.

HER SOLDIER

Day after day.
Night after night.
No sleeping at all.
She sits and she waits.
Around and around she twists her ring.
The photo she holds is damp from her tears.
Waiting and waiting.
Her life is on hold.
And though it has been weeks since he has called.
Maybe today.
Maybe today the phone will ring.
And though his last letter arrived weeks ago.
Maybe today.
Maybe today a letter will come.

She peeks through the space in the curtains.
The dark sedan drives slowly towards her.
The car stops at the curb.
They are so sorry.
They say he is lost.
It can't be true.
He went fighting for her.
His tour was done.
He was coming home.
But no one can find him.
He is missing in action.
But missing isn't dead.
And some things missing are found.
And so for her soldier she will wait.

VOICE MAIL

In my mind I see you.
Strong, healthy and happy.
You have left my world.
Gone to a place where my voice cannot reach you.
But your last voice mail is safely saved.
And I listen to your voice over and over.
Again and again I play your message.
I need so much to hear you say "Hi Sweetheart."
Friends tell me to delete the message.
It is only keeping the wound open.
But I never will.
I cannot.
For it is my last connection to you.

FANTASY

My heart beats in your chest.
I'm the center of your universe.
Your eyes search only for me in the crowd.
My smile is in your eyes.
My name is on your lips.
We keep no secrets.
No emotions hidden from each other.
I can stop searching for you.

WITHOUT YOU

My emotions are bruised.
A fractured heart carries a burden.
Shoulders hunched over.
Silently I wander.
Into this unfamiliar territory I'm plunged.
An unsettledness seeps into my very being.
I slip in and out of my new reality.
A last little star disappears from the night.
The sun rises in the morning sky.
Trees begin to make their shadows.
The petals of the flowers open and look upward.
Gardens still grow.
Books are written and read.
Music continues to play.
Songs are still sung.
People rush to get somewhere.
There are stones to turn over.
More mountains to climb.
A new day has begun.
How is this still possible without you?

GOODBYE KISS

What a gift to experience life.
To have your heart be so satisfied.
To feel the warmth of tears on your face.
Their saltiness touching your lips.
Your lover's touch.
The pause before your lips meet.
To miss someone so much.
Your heart shatters into pieces.

A WAKE

I'm just laying here.
Looking like I'm sleeping.
I'm dressed up in my best clothes.
And my bare toes.
This pillow is so soft.
The pink satin surrounds me.
The mahogany box is polished and so beautiful.
The scent of the flowers is overwhelming.
Look at all the people that have come to visit.
They came to see me one last time.
No more curtain calls.
Such kind words they are saying to me tonight.
I wonder why those words were never spoken before.
I would have benefited from knowing how they felt.
I felt the same way.

STIRRED BUT NOT SHAKEN

A moment of clarity.
A light bulb turned on.
Your hand reaching through the gloom.
Imagination or real?
I don't care.
Those sweet words.
That make you feel.
So hard to resist.
Or conceal.
Smoldering beneath the surface.
Dormant emotions flicker and intensify.
Ready to ignite.

THE WIDOW

The widow mourns.
Her lover's touch no longer hers.
She weeps.
No more secrets can he keep.
As she cries.
She wonders why.
Her eyes so sad.
For what they had.
In her mind she sees his face.
A vacant chair across the space.
Empty arms he used to fill.
His car keys on the windowsill.
Her lips that long to be kissed.
Oh his presence is so missed.
They used to dance.

No last chance.
A mandate of fate.
Alone she will wait.
On his grave she tends his flowers.
Toiling away many hours.
Alone in the yard.
She works so hard.
The pain so deep.
She cannot sleep.
A sense of dread.
That big cold bed.
As daylight grows dim.
She talks to him.
With no reply.
A heavy sigh.

THE GUIDE

Huddled on the ground you cried.
He picked you up.
You hadn't even heard him coming for you.
He tended to your skinned knees.
He mended your torn clothes.
He wiped the dirt, despair and tears from your face.
And spoke ever so kindly to you.
He cleared your guilty conscience.
And forgave it all.
He says he loves you.
You can't imagine why.
He turned you around.
And gently guided you in a different direction.
Walking with you silently.
He gave it all for you.
Someday he wants you back.

SEDUCTION

The heart feels what it will.
Luring you into love.
The illusion complete.
A ghost.
No apologies.
No excuses.
Wild abandon.
Caution to the wind.
No direction.
It drives its own course.
Creating a glow to follow.
The pull of a magnet.
It's a mystery.
Like a bee to honey.
It's a seduction.

IN THESE BROWN EYES

Powerful feelings are hidden.
Tears rest but must not fall.
A heart that sings but cannot be heard.
Words in a mouth that must never be spoken.
Lips that must stay sealed.

A SISTER

You see a resemblance to yourself.
She even talks a little like you do.
Mirrored mannerisms.
Matching moods.
A shared history.
Before the other speaks;
you know what they will say.
You laugh and cry at the same things.
A best friend.
A gift from your parents.
You share so much.
No time or distance can ever separate you.
She is always there for you.
There at the beginning;
with you at the end.
A sister.

BEGINNING AND END

Our hearts race.
You and me.
Me and you.
Wrapped up in each other.
Sharing the moonlight.
Or an unending horizon.
We imagine our future.
We reflect on our past.
Memories intertwined.
An enduring dream.
Feathered wings.
Embracing each experience.
Quietly shouldering the drama.
Simple and complicated.

Sometimes a stranger.
Sometimes a lover.
A gilded gift.
A vault of treasures.
Unable to tell where you end and I begin.
A living devotion.
Growing up.
Growing older.
Year after year.
Two chairs rocking in time.
Side by side the stones lay.
One name next to the other.
Seeing eternity together.

YOU

Your gaze falls on me.
And with that brief glimpse;
I disappear into the depths of your eyes.
I step into you.
I'm lost in that sweet swirl of emotions.
You are unaware that you carry me with you.
Of its own volition;
my hand reaches to hold your heart.
Today is the time we have to give.
What the heart feels cannot be explained.
Tomorrow my heart may break.
Be wounded and cast aside.
But it is no accident.
I was meant to share it with you.

GOING HOME

On tiptoes I stare over the precipice.
Tipping forward.
Arms stretched towards the stars.
Stepping on clouds.
Free falling to Heaven.
Sweet dreams.
A whispering voice.
The sound is so nice.
Strong arms reach through the dark.
Gathering me close.
Like a frayed favorite blanket.
Peace and quiet surround me.
I'm home.

LOST

Up or down.
Right or left.
No balance.
Trying and trying.
You don't even recognize yourself.
Missing.
Searching.
Running around in circles.
Seeking.
Looking and looking.
For who?
For what?
Around the next corner.
The bend in the road.
Your guiding light is too dim to see by.
The path you're walking is overgrown.
No bread crumbs left on the trail.

The way is unclear.
No markings to guide your way.
Can't go forward or back.
White to gray to black.
You wish for sleep that eludes you.
Thoughts you can't control.
Over and over you mind turns.
An unsettled sea of emotions.
Wishing and hoping.
Feelings twisted and tortured.
No sense in this time in this place.
Your hand reaches for another to hold.
With all your might you grasp to hold on.
You look and you look.
Nose pressed to the glass.
Only empty eyes stare back at you.
So lost.

IMAGINATION

I'm dialing the phone.
Holding the receiver to my ear.
I need to talk with you.
To hear your common sense.
To listen to your soothing, sing-song voice.
To hear you say I love you.
One more time.
And I'll say it back.
We'll probably both start crying.
You miss me.
I miss you more.
But I know the call will not go through.
It cannot.
And if by chance it did ring;
I know it could not be you on the other end.
That number is no longer yours.
So I'll imagine you answer.
And I'll start talking to you.
I know where to reach you.
You're at the little country cemetery.

TURTLE

People are like turtles.
We arm ourselves with a hard shell.
A soft underbelly.
Our heads tucked tight.
No sticking our necks out on the line.
We hide from the rest of the world.
Very slowly our legs propel us forward.
No one wants to be the one to run ahead.
To see what is out there.
Not alone.

RAINY DAY

April showers bring May flowers.
Only it is not April.
And this rain will not stop.
Day after day after day.
Noah, start gathering the animals.
Build that ark.
Gray and gloomy.
Drip.
Drop.
Drip.
Drop.
No break.
No blue sky in sight.
No sunshine peeking through.
The rivers rise.
Roads are flooded.

Bright orange cones block the way.
Heads are down.
Umbrellas up.
Tall rubber boots on every foot.
Ground saturated.
Puddles that no one jumps in.
New ponds to be named.
Basements leak.
Wind driven pellets hitting the windows.
Crying down the panes.
Aching bones.
Cold to the core.
A fire in the fireplace.
A hot cup of tea.
A really good book.
Nothing better on a rainy day.

THE STATE HOSPITAL

So sad.
To live.
If you can call it living.
And to die.
On the same piece of land.
Buried out back like an animal.
No name but a number.
A flat rock in the ground to remember you by.
The place with no birthdays.
No candles to mark your time here.
Not a real home.
Not with any of your family.
You were discarded.
Probably told it was for your own good.
They wouldn't be able to handle you.
It's for the best.

You would get the help you needed.

Out of sight.

Out of mind.

Strangers in white take care of your existence.

Their rubber soled shoes squeaking on the concrete.

They look through the window at you.

Locked up and medicated.

Ranting and raving.

Asking why.

Forgotten.

Discarded.

Put away.

Out of sight of the real people.

Of which you are not considered one.

Did you wonder why were you born into this world?

What was your purpose?

MAMMOGRAM

Mammogram last week.
No time to wait for the results.
The holidays are right around the corner.
Too busy.
Things to do.
You think you are in the clear.
The weekend passes.
You haven't felt sick.
Nothing out of the ordinary.
Monday comes.
The phone rings.
Something was on that last film.
Though they can't say what it is.
They want you to come back.
Take some more films.
You wait for that appointment.
Scared to death.
Can time move any slower?

What if it's cancer?

Oh I don't want to imagine.

Don't even think that way.

Redo films.

Wait, wait, wait.

Don't make eye contact with the other ladies waiting.

All of us wearing our tie back pajama tops.

Eat the crackers.

Have a juice.

Wait, wait, wait some more.

The flower smocked nurse appears.

Your name is called.

You are pulled away from the group.

All eyes follow you to the doorway.

She smiles.

You are okay.

This time.

LETTER FROM BEN

White lined school paper.
Rough and tattered on the edges.
Two different colors of ink.
Twenty lines of writing.
From three thousand miles away.
One I love you.
A message for me.
From your heart to mine.
This precious gift.
A tiny piece of heaven.
For me to hold in my hands.
A treasure.

ANOTHER DAY

Another day is done.
The night has begun.
The purple twilight has seeped out of the sky.
I pull my nightgown over my head.
My back is to the mirror.
I can't stand to see my body naked.
I feel exposed and vulnerable.
The little night light glows in the darkness.
Quiet now the house rests.
I feel my way to my room.
Slip into bed.
I turn on my side and pull the covers over my head.
Snuggled and cozy.
I put my hands together to pray.
Night after night the same prayers go up.
And every night as I pray I fall asleep.
Never getting to finish what I need to say.
Morning comes and I feel the loss.
I'll try to stay awake longer tonight.

FORBIDDEN

My heart is being tugged on.
Pulled in a direction I cannot follow.
Taken somewhere I must not go.
Forbidden.
Oh the temptation is great.
And I am weak.
Why do you get me?
I don't know how this is possible.
I don't know myself half the time.
With you I am special.
Not an inconvenience.

HERE

Love life.
Live life.
You're here.
Then you're not.

BROKEN

Shattered.
Scattered
Bits and pieces.
Here and there.
Sharp edges.
Destroyed.
Worthless.
Swept aside.
Discarded.
Thrown away.

ONE YEAR

It is almost a year since you left me.
Sometimes I think I hear you call my name.
I can see your smile.
And hear your laugh.
You whisper that everything is okay.
I can feel your gentle touch.
Your arms wrapped around me.
One year.
A lot has changed and then again nothing.
Still here.
Same place.
Same thoughts.
Doing the same things.
Over and over.
Day in and day out.
Wish you were here.
Missing you.

MISS YOU

Miss you.
Miss you.
Wish I could kiss you.
What is it like there?
Can you see me?
Do you hear my thoughts?
I think about you every day.
There is so much I want to share with you.
We wasted a lot of time being so far apart.
Telephone calls put off until later.
Some time more convenient.
Now it is too late.
You are gone.
And I'm still here.
Missing you.
Missing you.
Wish I were kissing you.

FAVORITE PHOTO

That's my favorite photo.
The little one in the gold frame.
The little girl with her big sister.
The little girl with the twinkly brown eyes.
The little girl with the over the top spirit.
Free and flying.
The little girl with the crooked smile.
She believed that the world was hers.
But it didn't last.
Why wasn't she good enough the way she was?
Why must her spirit be broken?
Trampled, torn and bruised.
Those words hurt her so deeply.
And she learned to inflict that hurt back.
She felt shamed and humiliated.
She eventually hated herself.
Day by day she went deeper and deeper inside herself.
Some place where the hurt couldn't reach her.
The happy little girl disappeared.
Going.
Going.
Gone.

BEST FRIEND

So happy that in this life our paths have crossed.
I cannot imagine not having you in my life.
And if we had not met;
forever I would wonder why I was not deemed worthy.
To have a best friend.
To be a best friend.
A kindred spirit.
A bosom buddy.
But you called.
You knew I needed you.
And here we are.
My dear sweet friend.
Together at last.

HOPE

We can't live without it.
It makes life livable.
Nothing matters without it.
We long for it.
It makes being alive tolerable.
We hope for love.
We hope for peace.
We hope for laughter.
We hope for a brighter tomorrow.
We hope for what we thought we once had.
We hope for innocence.
We hope for the same things.
We fight for hope.

CLAWS

I don't know when this anger
and rage crept into me.
No more sweetness and light.
I'm so defensive.
Ready to pounce.
To claw your eyes out.
To rip you apart.
Piece by piece.
Until you are a bone.
A carcass.
Then there is nothing.
Nothing more I can take from you.

A SIGN

Early for an appointment.
I'm sitting on a bench.
Waiting and watching people.
One by one they walk past me.
No one has smiled.
Not one person.
Walking fast.
Heads down.
No eye contact.
No hellos.
I'm invisible.
No optimism in sight.
Until now.
A little girl in cowgirl boots jumping up and down.
Spinning and twirling.
Finally.
A sign of happiness.
The first sign of hope.
It still exists.
It's a start.

SAD GIRL

Can you see me?
I feel invisible.
Talk to me.
Look me in the eyes.
Hello, I'm here.
When did I become so alone?
I must have been looking away when you left my side?
Confidence gone.
No longer mine.
Fearful.
Not belonging.
Searching still.
Cowered in the corner watching.
Maybe I'll cry myself to sleep.
I'll wake up and start waiting.
For what I can't imagine.
Sad girl.

SEE ME

Hold my hand.
Make me happy for a while.
Sweet.
Light.
Full of promise.
Hope.
Joy.
See me for me.
See past my anger.
My mind is dark right now.
You know that's not me.
Not who I really am.
You know me.

HER SAD SEASON

It has been four weeks.
This is a nightmare her eyes cannot open from.
Her support system failing.
She needs them more than ever.
Her own flesh and blood abandon her.
They have left her high and dry.
Written off and discarded as damaged goods.
They do not believe in her.
Cruel words meant to inflict the most damage.
A closed fist of thrown words.
Almost worse than the initial bruising blow.
And yet she tries her best.
Like a wind-up toy.
On and on she goes.
Doing what needs to be done.

She continues to make a holiday to share.
Christmas is days away.
Just around the corner.
Twinkling the tree sits.
It's skirt bearing their gifts.
High above the angel looks down with sadness.
Tears on her porcelain face.
The spiral ham is ready to be the center of the feast.
No cold air being let in as they arrive.
No hands being warmed up in front of the fire.
No laughing.
No talking over one another needing to be heard.
No one is coming.
No one is leaving.
They are already gone.

THE MOMENT

It is hard to stay in the moment.
To enjoy this minute.
Nothing more.
No planning.
No to do lists.
No should haves.
To just be.
No one to impress at this moment.
To sit and relax.
To feel the sunshine through the closed winter window.
To not be in the rat race for a moment.
To listen to the birds singing.
A moment when nothing is expected of you.
You are alive.
Close your eyes.
Listen to your body.
Hear the blood rushing through your veins.
Be in the moment.
After all, isn't that all we have?
At the moment.

HOLD ME

Oh these aching arms that long to hold you.
To hold you tightly against me.
As close as I can.
For as long as I can.
To feel your body's warmth.
I want nothing more.
Nothing but that basic contact.
Nothing.
That is enough.

LOVE?

You think you love me.
You say it all the time.
But I can't believe you.
I don't feel it.
I don't feel like that special one.
I want to.
But it's just words.
You don't know me anymore.
You have nothing to say to me.
Only small talk.
No secrets for us to keep.
Nothing about us.
What a waste.
You don't know what I need.
I've even told you.

Several times.

It's not a lot.

Hold my hand.

Touch my face.

Touch my heart.

Reach for me without asking for something in return.

It seemed we had so much more in the beginning.

We were a team.

You and me.

Such promise.

Now you don't know why my heart keeps beating.

You don't know my dreams.

And I guess I don't know yours.

I imagined our love growing differently.

Didn't you?

CHILD'S SPIRIT

How lucky are those that reach adulthood with their
child's spirit still intact.
Their eyes full of wonder.
A heart that is full of hope.
For most will arrive at that threshold with their spirit
somewhat damaged.
Some spirits will be so tarnished that they cannot see a
way in this world.
They spout doom and gloom.
Those are the poor me's.
 I'm owed this.
 I deserve that.
Some will have had the spirit beaten out of them.
Others may have a punctured spirit.
And for a time they can cover the hole.
But, eventually the patch lifts.

And down they spiral.

They are in a flux of happy or sad.

Those whose spirits remain intact see the light in our world.

They see the blue in the sky.

They paint the world with a colorful brush.

They hear the joyful noises.

Not the agonizing cries.

They play.

Their innocent eyes still see the good in mankind.

Their optimism is unwavering.

Their wings are still securely attached.

Not shredded or missing.

They delight in just being alive and living.

They lift us all up.

They give us hope.

EMPTY WISH

Mind always racing.
Random thoughts.
Nothing organized.
Going from one idea to another.
Going a hundred miles an hour.
No rhyme.
No reason.
Racing.
Do this.
No that.
Now.
Later.
Never.
A life with no living.
A closet full of clothes and nothing to wear.
Two eyes that see nothing.
Ears that don't listen.
Too much doesn't make sense.
Torn in two.
Pulled in different directions.
A wish bone with no wish.

SKIN

With skin so thin.
A thoughtless word pierces like a spear.
It tears through without a thought.

REGRETS

Whose life are you living?
Is it what you imagined long ago?
Are you happy?
Do you feel like you are watching your life through
someone else's eyes?
Do you ever stare off and wonder how you got
here?
To this point in your life.
What the hell happened?
Must have been some crazy stuff.
How many hearts did you damage to get here?
Was it worth it?
Regret.
Small word.
Big meaning.
There is not a person alive without regrets.
A liar if they say otherwise.
Do you ever think about what you gave away?
Mangled and left by the side of the road.
Crying and crying.
Begging you to stay.
To come back.
And you just kept going.
Heartless.

Selfish to the core.
Thinking only of yourself.
Ignoring what you had.
All you had said.
All you had promised.
God, what was wrong with you?
Hope torn away.
A future killed.
I just left.
In my mind I never went back.
That's a lie.
What do you do now?
And you wondering what you did wrong.
What could you do to change my mind?
Before it's too late.
It's too late.
When it wasn't you at all.
It wasn't your fault.
It wasn't you that messed up.
It wasn't you that broke us.
It wasn't you.
It was me.
With regrets.

ROBOTS

Our daily lives are so programmed.
Robots with beating hearts.
Wake up.
Maybe exercise.
Maybe not.
Shower.
Hair and makeup.
Get dressed.
Eat breakfast.
Work.
Eat lunch.
Work some more.
Eat dinner.
Maybe exercise.
Maybe not.
Relax.
Read.
Watch TV.
Bed.
Begin again.
And on and on it goes.
And where it stops nobody knows.

CAGED

You feel like you are in a cage with no bars.
You can only go so far.
And then you hit the wall.
You live your life in a corner.
Never venturing too far outside the comfort zone.
Some days you may feel bold and brave.
You feel like you could do anything.
Hop in the car and just keep driving and driving.
Far beyond the horizon.
You could start over.
Where nobody knows you.
You could be whole there.
A new beginning.
You think that could work.
But the old baggage would weigh you down.
It would catch up with you.
It's a chain around your ankles.
Your wrists are tied.
No escaping it.
It follows you.
It's your personal prison.

SAD SMILE

What a sad smile.
It doesn't reach your eyes.
No crinkling at the corners.
You really are trying though.
But there is no laughter.
No twinkle in those eyes.
So much fear.
You are afraid to live.
To live might mean getting slapped back down.
The pain could start over.
You couldn't take that again.
Better to just lay low.
Stay beneath the radar.
You think too much.
Around and around your thoughts go.
Whirling faster and faster in that head of yours.
Tripping and tumbling over each other.
Are you equally as afraid to die?
You are out of control.
You know it.
Your family knows it.
You can't enjoy what should cause you so much joy.
I'm so sorry for you.
Will you ever be better?

OCEAN

Throughout eternity.
Waves roll in and peel back out.
Cold salty water.
Depositing gifts of shells and sea glass.
Leaving a white crooked line where it has been.
The sound is mesmerizing.
Seducing us to sleep.
Rocking boats back and forth.
Making ledges and edges in the packed sand.
Cutting into dunes.
Dragging tall sea grass back to the depths.
Back to where the mermaids swim.
Washing away our footsteps;
as if we never existed.

CHRISTMAS CHAOS

Christmas songs sometimes make me cry.

Family missed.

Old traditions remembered.

Loved ones gone.

Homesick.

Heartbroken.

Are there enough presents for everyone?

Equal amounts.

Not too much for one.

Too little for another.

There is so much to do.

The perfect presents to buy and then wrap.

The crowds to endure.

The lines to wait in.

Little children sitting on the lap of Santa Claus.

They shouldn't talk to strangers.

And then we tell them to sit on Santa's lap.

What is that about?

That makes no sense.

Cookies to be baked.

But not by me.

Thanks Mom.

The decorations to be put up inside and out.

Lights to be lit.

It's so cold outside.

Wet crusty mittens to dry.

Frozen fingers and toes.

The wait for the car heater to work.

The cards to write.

The party to plan.

Invitations to send out.

Lists to be made and changed over and over.

Clean that house top to bottom.

Special foods to prepare.

The weight to lose to fit into that perfect outfit.

Air kisses on every cheek.

It never ends.

Why do we set expectations we can never meet?

Something doesn't make sense.

I'm not a Scrooge.

I'm just asking the question.

What is the real meaning of Christmas?

I think we've whipped and twisted ourselves into
believing it is something it is not.

I'm with you Charlie Brown I just don't get it.

PRETENDING

A foot or two separates them.
But it might as well be a million miles.
Hearts that ache with the distance.
An unspoken need.
They know it is wrong to feel this way.
The urge to reach out.
A yearning to possess.
Bewitched and mesmerized.
Loyalties elsewhere.
Others are waiting.
Off limits.
A conflict of emotions.
Wistful reflection.
A restrained infatuation.
An unblemished desire.

Virtuous temptation.
Nothing can ever happen.
Controlled feelings that can go nowhere.
Hidden away from the light of day.
Even from each other.
They share their stories.
So much alike.
Fun to be together.
And torture at the same time.
Platonic and proper.
An innocent touch.
A chaste hug.
Nothing more.
Pretending.

STUFF

Are you driven by money and status?
Wearing designer clothes and driving luxury cars.
You must be seen with the "right" people.
Your jewelry must be the real thing.
Short on compassion for others?
Try and remember this:
You start out wearing a bib.
And you end up wearing a bib.
You start out wearing a diaper.
And you end up wearing a diaper.
What goes around comes around.
The rest is just stuff.

Breinigsville, PA USA
24 March 2011
258404BV00001B/5/P